the
ULTIMATE
series

PIANO · VOCAL · GUITAR

the new Love and Wedding songbook

This publication is not for sale in
the EC and/or Australia
or New Zealand.

HAL·LEONARD®
CORPORATION

7777 W. BLUEMOUND RD. P.O. BOX 13819 MILWAUKEE, WI 53213

the new Love and Wedding songbook

AIR
(from Water Music Suite)

Slowly and stately

G. F. HANDEL

AND I LOVE HER

Words and Music by JOHN LENNON
and PAUL McCARTNEY

ALL THE WAY

Words by SAMMY CAHN
Music by JAMES VAN HEUSEN

When some-bod-y loves you, it's no good un-less he loves you
When some-bod-y needs you, it's no good un-less she needs you

all the way.
all the way.

Hap-py to be near you, when you need some-one to cheer you
Thru the good or lean years and for all the in be-tween years,

all the way.
come what may.

Tall-er_____ than the tall-est tree is,
Who knows_____ where the road will lead us,

ANNIVERSARY SONG

By AL JOLSON
and SAUL CHAPLIN

Moderately Slow

Oh! _____ how we danced _____ on the
Night _____ seemed to fade _____ in - to

night _____ we were wed _____ We
blos - som - ing down _____ The

vowed _____ our true love _____ though a
sun _____ shone a - new _____ but the

12

THE ANNIVERSARY WALTZ

Words and Music by AL DUBIN
& DAVE FRANKLIN

ped.

AVE MARIA

Very slowly

Music by FRANZ SCHUBERT
Traditional liturgical text

A - ve Ma - ri - a! gra - ti - a* ple -

na, Ma - ri - a, gra - ti - a

ple - na, Ma - ri - a, gra - ti - a ple -

*pronounced grah - tsee - ah

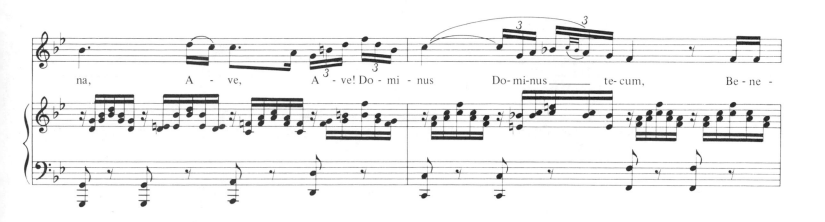

na, A - ve, A - ve! Do - mi - nus Do - mi - nus _____ te - cum, Be - ne -

di - cta tu in mu - li - e - ri-bus, et be - ne - di - ctus, et

be - ne - di - ctus fru - ctus ven - tris, ven- tris, tu - i, Je - sus.**

A - ve Ma - ri - a!

** pronounced yeh - zoos

To Coda ⊕

ho - ra mor - tis no strae,　　　in　　ho - ra mor - tis, mor - tis no - strae,　　　　in

ho - ra mor - tis no - strae.　　　A - ve Ma - ri -

D.S. al Coda

a!

⊕ CODA

dim.

BECAUSE

Words by EDWARD TESCHEMACHER
Music by GUY D' HARDELOT

BRIDAL CHORUS

(From "Lohengrin")

RICHARD WAGNER

CANDLE ON THE WATER

(From Walt Disney Productions' "PETE'S DRAGON")

Words and Music by AL KASHA
and JOEL HIRSCHHORN

I'll be your can-dle on the wa-ter,   My love for you will al-ways
I'll be your can-dle on the wa-ter,   'Til ev-'ry wave is warm and

burn.   I know you're lost   and drift-ing,   But the clouds are lift-ing,
bright,   My soul is there   be-side you,   Let this can-dle guide you

don't give up you have some-where to turn.
soon you'll see a gold-en stream of   light.

CANON IN D

Johann Pachelbel
Arranged by MARION VERHAALEN

CAN'T HELP FALLING IN LOVE

Words and Music by
GEORGE DAVID WEISS, HUGO PERETTI,
and LUIGI CREATORE

COULD I HAVE THIS DANCE

Words and Music by
WAYLAND HOLYFIELD and BOB HOUSE

Moderately Slow

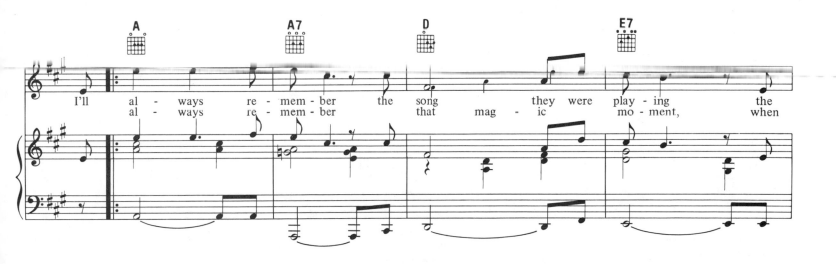

I'll al-ways re-mem-ber the song they were play-ing, the
al-ways re-mem-ber that mag-ic mo-ment, when

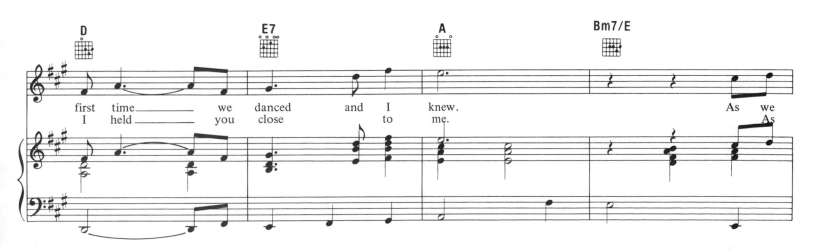

first time_____ we danced and I knew.
I held_____ you close to me.

As we
As

CAN'T SMILE WITHOUT YOU

Moderately, with a relaxed beat

Words and Music by CHRIS ARNOLD,
DAVID MARTIN and GEOFF MORROW

EMBRACEABLE YOU

Words by IRA GERSHWIN
Music by GEORGE GERSHWIN

Doz-ens of girls would storm___ up; I had to lock my door.

Some-how I could-n't warm___ up to one be-fore.

What was it that con-trolled___ me? What kept my love life lean? My in-tu-i-tion told___

FALLING IN LOVE WITH LOVE

(From "THE BOYS FROM SYRACUSE")

Words by LORENZ HART
Music by RICHARD RODGERS

ENDLESS LOVE

Words and Music by
LIONEL RICHIE

AN EVERLASTING LOVE

Words and Music by
BARRY GIBB

FEELINGS
(¿DIME?)

English Words and Music by MORRIS ALBERT
Spanish Lyric by THOMAS FUNDORA

THE FIRST TIME EVER I SAW YOUR FACE

Words and Music by
EWAN MacCOLL

FOR ALL WE KNOW
(From the Motion Picture "LOVERS AND OTHER STRANGERS")

Words by ROBB WILSON and JAMES GRIFFIN
Music by FRED KARLIN

Moderato, with a light beat

Love,_____ look at the two of us,_____ Stran-

gers_____ in man-y ways._____

FOREVER AND EVER, AMEN

Words and Music by DON SCHLITZ
and PAUL OVERSTREET

MCA MUSIC PUBLISHING

THE HAWAIIAN WEDDING SONG

English Words by AL HOFFMAN & DICK MANNING
Hawaiian Words & Music by CHARLES E. KING

Slowly, with much warmth

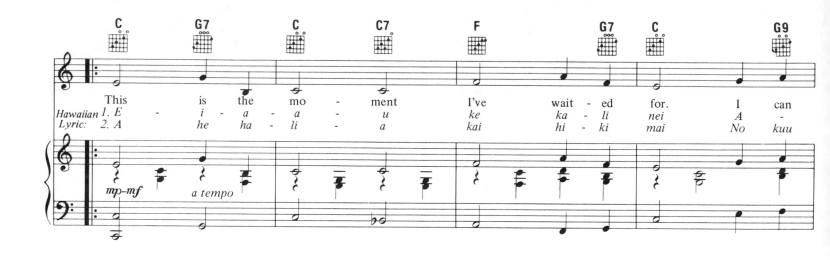

This is the mo- ment I've wait- ed for. I can

Hawaiian 1. E - i - a - a - u ke ka - li nei I A

Lyric: 2. A he ha - li - a kai hi - ki mai No kuu

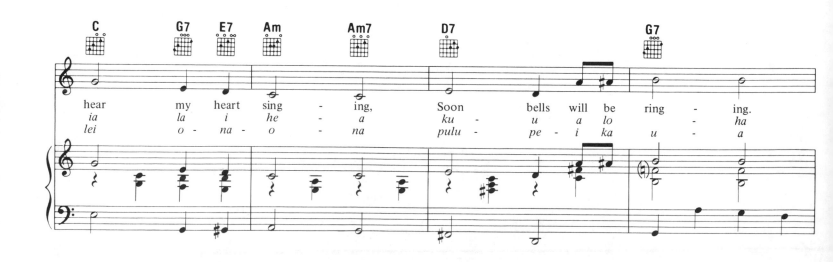

hear my heart sing- ing, Soon bells will be ring- ing.

ia la i he - a ku - u a lo - ha

lei o - na - o - na pulu- pe - i ka u - a

HOW DEEP IS YOUR LOVE

Words and Music by BARRY GIBB,
ROBIN GIBB and MAURICE GIBB

HERE, THERE AND EVERYWHERE

Words and Music by JOHN LENNON
and PAUL McCARTNEY

HOPELESSLY DEVOTED TO YOU

Words and Music by
JOHN FARRAR

I JUST FALL IN LOVE AGAIN

Words and Music by
LARRY HERBSTRITT, STEPHEN H. DORFF,
GLORIA SKLEROV and HARRY LLOYD

I LOVE YOU

Words and Music by
COLE PORTER

I LOVE YOU TRULY

I ONLY HAVE EYES FOR YOU

Written by AL DUBIN
and HARRY WARREN

91

I PLEDGE MY LOVE

Words by DINO FEKARIS
Music by DINO FEKARIS and FREDDIE PERREN

Ooh, ooh, ooh, ooh, wee, ooh, al-ways to-geth-er, to-geth-er for-ev-er,

al-ways to-geth-er for-ev-er. I will love you 'til the day I die.___ I know this now and my love won't run dry.___

You came a-long, my life has be-gun; Two hearts are now beat-ing as though they were one.___

I WANT YOU, I NEED YOU, I LOVE YOU

Words by MAURICE MYSELS
Music by IRA KOSLOFF

Moderately Slow

Hold me close, __ hold me tight; __ make me thrill __ with de-light. Let me know __ where I stand __ from the start. _____ I Want You, I Need You, I Love You _____ with all my heart. __ Ev-'ry time _____ that you're near __ all my cares _____ dis-ap-pear. __ Dar-ling,

I'LL HAVE TO SAY I LOVE YOU IN A SONG

Words and Music by JIM CROCE

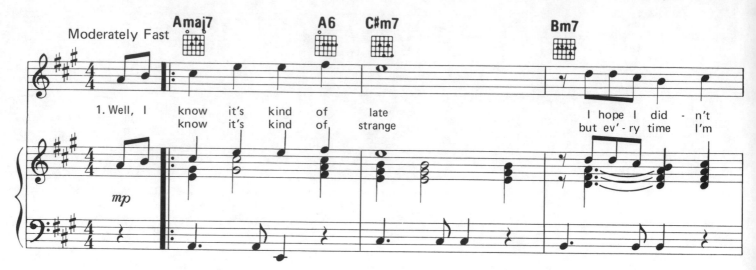

1. Well, I know it's kind of late
know it's kind of strange
I hope I did - n't
but ev' - ry time I'm

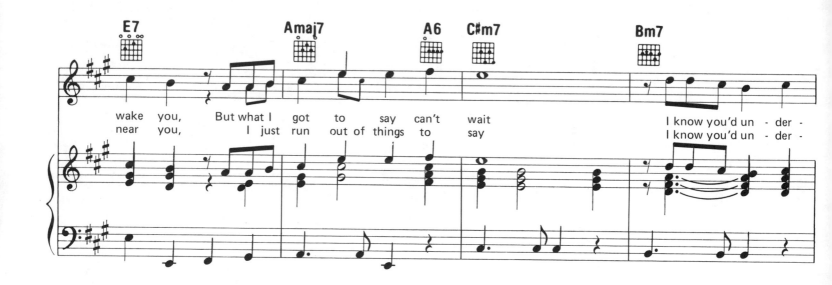

wake you, But what I got to say can't wait
near you, I just run out of things to say
I know you'd un - der -
I know you'd un - der -

stand.___
stand.___

1,2,4. Ev' - ry time I tried to tell___ you the words just came out
3. Ev' - ry time the time was right___ all the words just came out

I'M CONFESSIN'
(THAT I LOVE YOU)

By AL NEIBURG, DOC DOUGHERTY
and ELLIS REYNOLDS

IF WE ONLY HAVE LOVE

English lyrics by
MORT SHUMAN and ERIC BLAU
Original French lyrics by JACQUES BREL
Music by JACQUES BREL

JESU, JOY OF MAN'S DESIRING

By J.S. BACH

106

Ho - ly wis - dom,
Hark, what peace - ful

love____ most____ bright,
mu - sic____ rings,

Drawn   by
Where   the

known,
own,

Soar   In - ing the

dy - ing   round____ Thy____   throne.
love   of   joys____ un -   known.

JUST THE WAY YOU ARE

Words and Music by
BILLY JOEL

Don't go chang-ing ___ to try and please me ___ You nev-er

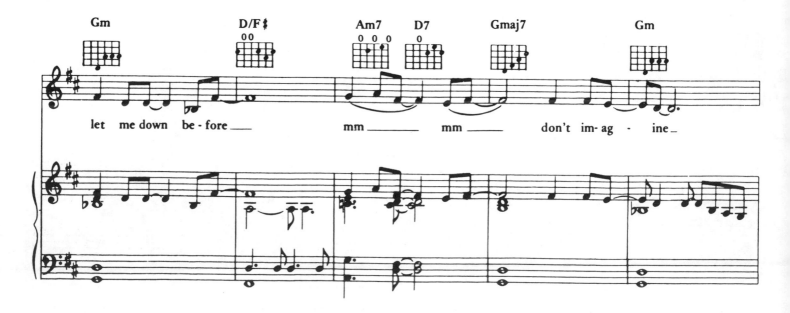

let me down be-fore ___ mm ___ mm ___ don't im-ag - ine _

LONGER

Words and Music by
DAN FOGELBERG

Moderate Ballad

Long - er than____ there've been fish - es in the o - cean,
Strong - er than____ an - y moun - tain cath - e - dral.
Through the years____ as the fi - re starts to mel - low,

THE LAST TIME I FELT LIKE THIS

(From the Universal Picture "Same Time, Next Year")

Words by ALAN BERGMAN
and MARILYN BERGMAN
Music by MARVIN HAMLISCH

Hel - lo, I don't_ e - ven know_ your name, but I'm hop-in' all__ the
lo, I can't_wait till we're_ a - lone, some - where qui-et on__ our

same this is more than just a sim - ple hel - lo. Hel - lo, do I smile and walk__ a-
own so that we can fall the rest of the way. I know that be - fore the night__ is

way? No, I think I'll smile_ and stay to see where this might_ go.
thru, I'll be talk - ing love_ to you, mean - ing ev - 'ry word I____ say.

'Cause The Last Time I Felt Like This

LET ME CALL YOU SWEETHEART
(I'm In Love With You)

Words by BETH SLATER WHITSON
Music by LEO FRIEDMAN

Let Me Call You Sweet - heart, I'm in love with you. Let me hear you whis - per that you

THE LORD'S PRAYER

By ALBERT HAY MALOTTE

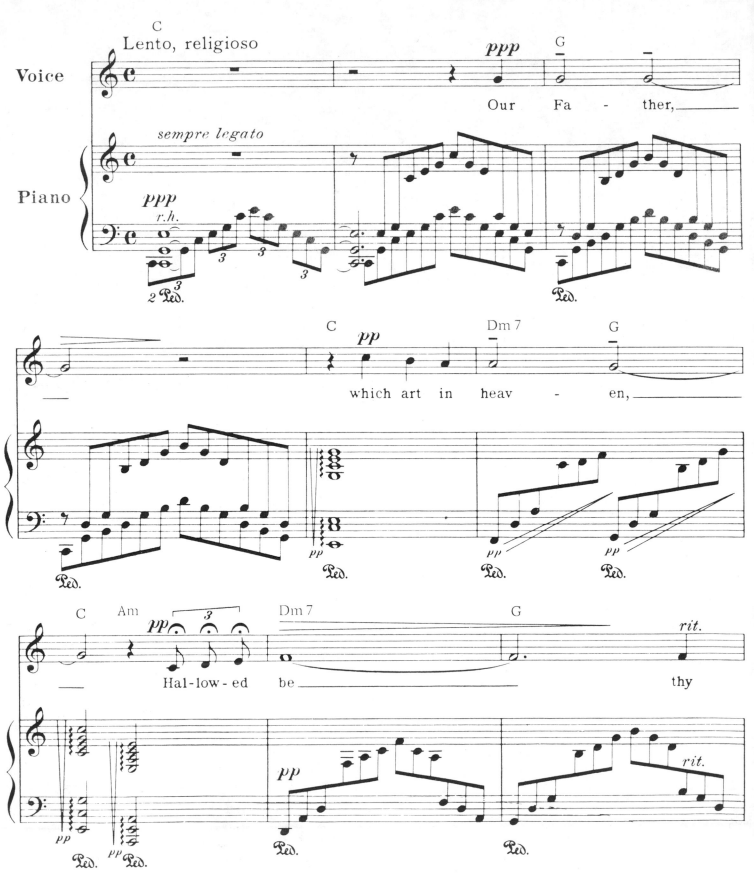

THE LOVE INSIDE

Words and Music by
BARRY GIBB

132

L-O-V-E

Words and Music by WAYNE DOUGLAS, JR.

LOVE IS FOREVER

Words and Music by WAYNE BRATHWAITE,
BARRY J. EASTMOND and BILLY OCEAN

I re-live the same old dream day and night,
With ev-'ry pass-ing day I re-a-lize

mem-o-ries of love I knew.
that time will ne-ver heal the pain.

LOVE IS A SIMPLE THING

Words by JUNE CARROLL
Music by ARTHUR SIEGEL

Moderate (Rocking Tempo)

Love Is A Sim-ple Thing,

Love is a sil-ver ring, Shi-ny as a rib-bonbow, soft as a qui-et snow.

Love is a nur-ser-y rhyme, Old as the tick of time.

Love is so man-y things, bright as an an-gel's wings, Gen-tle as the morn-ing light,

LOVE IS HERE TO STAY
(From GOLDWYN FOLLIES)

Words by IRA GERSHWIN
Music by GEORGE GERSHWIN

LOVE ME TENDER

Words and Music by ELVIS PRESLEY
and VERA MATSON

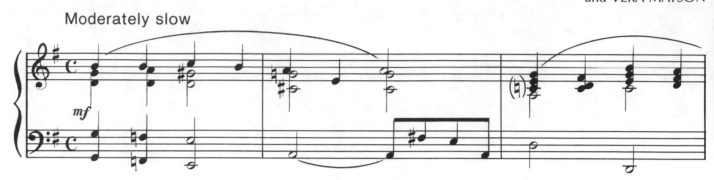

1. Love Me Ten - der, love me sweet;
2. Love Me Ten - der, love me long;
3. Love Me Ten - der, love me dear;

Nev - er let me go.
Take me to your heart.
Tell me you are mine.

You have made my
For it's there that
I'll be yours through

EXTRA VERSE 4. When at last my dreams come true,
Darling, this I know:
Happiness will follow you
Everywhere you go.

LOVE THEME FROM FLASHDANCE

Music by GIORGIO MORODER

Moderately slow

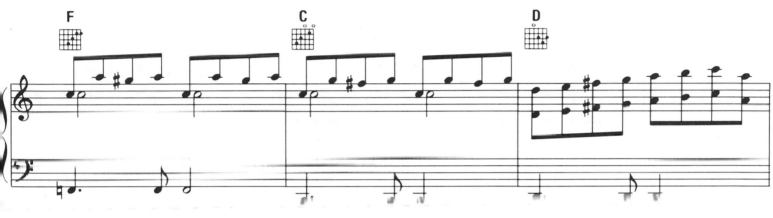

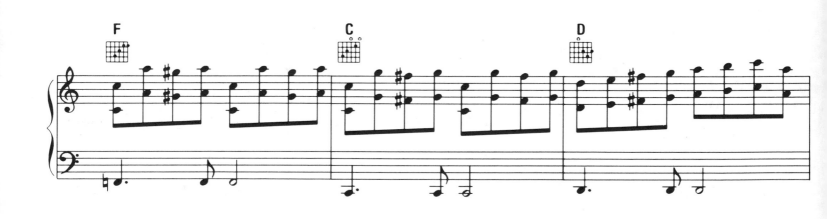

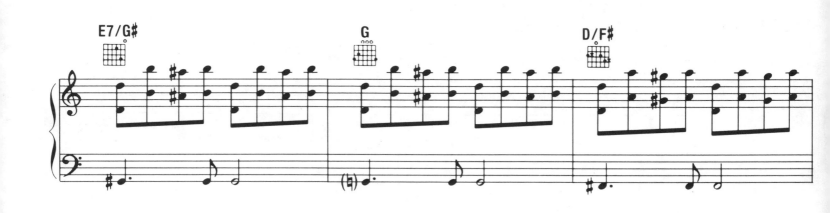

LOVE'S GROWN DEEP

Words and Music by
KENNY NOLAN

MAY YOU ALWAYS

Words and Music by
LARRY MARKES and DICK CHARLES

1. May You Al-ways walk in sun-shine, slum-ber warm when night winds blow. May You Al-ways
2. May good for-tune find your door-way, may the blue-bird sing your song. May no trou-ble
3. May You Al-ways be a dream-er, may your wild-est dream come true. May you find some

live with laugh-ter for a smile be-comes you so

stay too long. May your heart-aches

be for-got-ten, may no tears be spilled. May old ac-quaint-ance be re-mem-bered,

and your cup of kind ness filled, and   one to love as much as I love you.

MEET ME TONIGHT IN DREAMLAND

Words by BETH SLATER WHITSON
Music by LEO FRIEDMAN

MISTY

Words by JOHNNY BURKE
Music by ERROLL GARNER

MY CUP RUNNETH OVER

(From "I DO! I DO!")

Words by TOM JONES
Music by HARVEY SCHMIDT

MY FUNNY VALENTINE

(From "BABES IN ARMS")

Words by LORENZ HART
Music by RICHARD RODGERS

NIGHT AND DAY

Words and Music by
COLE PORTER

NO OTHER LOVE

(From "ME AND JULIET")

Words by OSCAR HAMMERSTEIN II
Music by RICHARD RODGERS

ODE TO JOY

Music by LUDWIG VAN BEETHOVEN
Words adapted from FRIEDRICH SCHILLER

Moderately

Sing to joy and glad-ness now and ev-er-more to free-dom's song:

O-pen up our heart's de-sire with love that's ev-er-last-ing.

Let this mag-ic bring to-geth-er all who dwell up-on the earth. All

OH, PROMISE ME!

Words by CLEMENT SCOTT
Music by REGINALD de KOVEN

ONE HAND, ONE HEART

(From "WEST SIDE STORY")

Lyrics by STEPHEN SONDHEIM
Music by LEONARD BERNSTEIN

184

PEOPLE WILL SAY WE'RE IN LOVE
(From "OKLAHOMA!")

Words by OSCAR HAMMERSTEIN II
Music by RICHARD RODGERS

SECRET LOVE

Lyric by PAUL FRANCIS WEBSTER
Music by SAMMY FAIN

Once I had a se-cret love That lived with-in the heart of me, All too soon my se-cret love Be-came im-pa-tient to be

So I told a friend-ly star, The way that dream-ers oft-en do, Just how won-der-ful you are And why I'm so in love with

SEPTEMBER MORN

Words and Music by NEIL DIAMOND
and GILBERT BECAUD

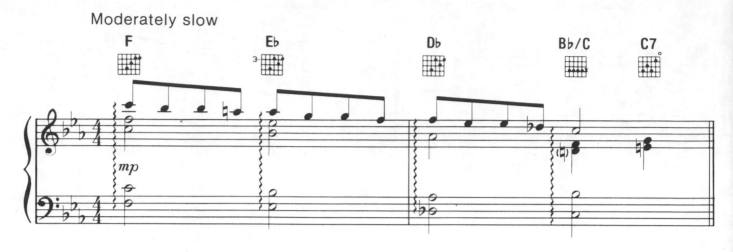

Moderately slow

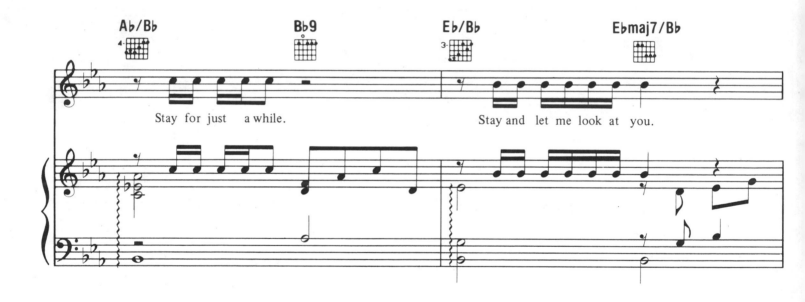

Stay for just a while.

Stay and let me look at you.

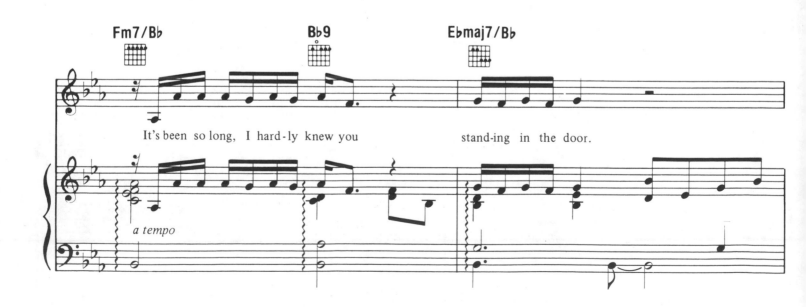

It's been so long, I hard-ly knew you

stand-ing in the door.

SHADOWS IN THE MOONLIGHT

Words and Music by
CHARLIE BLACK and RORY BOURKE

SO IN LOVE

(From "KISS ME KATE")

Words and Music by COLE PORTER

love   with   you,   my   love_____   am

SOME ENCHANTED EVENING

(From "SOUTH PACIFIC")

Words by OSCAR HAMMERSTEIN II
Music by RICHARD RODGERS

SOMEWHERE
(From "WEST SIDE STORY")

Lyrics by STEPHEN SONDHEIM
Music by LEONARD BERNSTEIN

SUNRISE, SUNSET
(From the Musical "FIDDLER ON THE ROOF")

Words by SHELDON HARNICK
Music by JERRY BOCK

213

THIS I PROMISE YOU

Words and Music by CLYDE OTIS
and VINCENT CORSO

THESE ARE THE BEST TIMES

Words and Music by SHANE TATUM

THROUGH THE YEARS

Words and Music by
STEVE DORFF and MARTY PANZER

Appreciatively

THE TIES THAT BIND

Words and Music by CLYDE OTIS
and VIN CORSO

TILL

Words by CARL SIGMAN
Music by CHARLES DANVERS

Moderately

Till the moon de - serts the sky

Till all the seas run dry Till then I'll wor - ship you. Till

TILL THE END OF TIME
(Based On Chopin's Polonaise)

Words and Music by BUDDY KAYE
and TED MOSSMAN

Slowly, with expression

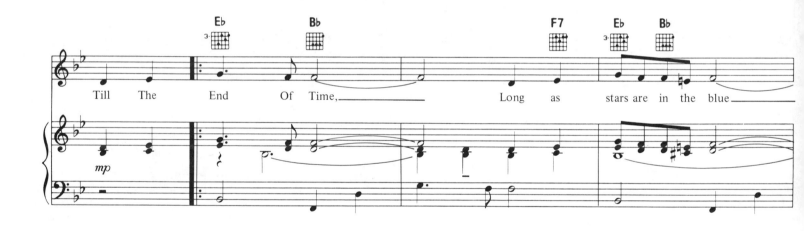

Till The End Of Time,_____ Long as stars are in the blue_____

Long as there's a spring, a bird to sing I'll go on lov-ing

234

TO LOVE AGAIN
(Theme From "The Eddy Duchin Story")
Based on Chopin's E flat Nocturne

Words by NED WASHINGTON
Music by MORRIS STOLOFF & GEORGE SIDNEY

TIME AFTER TIME

Words and Music by CYNDI LAUPER
and ROB HYMAN

TOO MUCH HEAVEN

Words and Music by BARRY GIBB,
ROBIN GIBB and MAURICE GIBB

No-bod-y gets too much heav-en no more, it's much hard-er to come by; I'm wait-ing in line. _____ No-bod-y gets too much

TURN AROUND

Words and Music by NEIL DIAMOND,
BURT BACHARACH and CAROLE BAYER SAGER

TRUE LOVE

Moderately Slow

Words and Music by
COLE PORTER

TRUMPET TUNE

JEREMIAH CLARKE

TRUMPET VOLUNTARY

JEREMIAH CLARKE

TRY TO REMEMBER
(From "THE FANTASTICKS")

Words by TOM JONES
Music by HARVEY SCHMIDT

Slowly, with tenderness

WEDDING PROCESSIONAL
(From "The Sound Of Music")

Words by OSCAR HAMMERSTEIN II
Music by RICHARD RODGERS

Majestically

For the entrance of the Bride

WHEN I FALL IN LOVE

Words by EDWARD HEYMAN
Music by VICTOR YOUNG

Slowly, with much feeling

When I fall in love it will be for-ev-er, or I'll nev-er fall in love._____ In a rest-less world like this is, love is end-ed be-fore it's be-gun, and too man-y moon-light kiss-es seem to

WEDDING MARCH

FELIX MENDELSSOHN

Majestically

WHEN I NEED YOU

Moderately, with feeling

Words by CAROLE BAYER SAGER
Music by ALBERT HAMMOND

WHITHER THOU GOEST

Words and Music by
GUY SINGER

WITH THIS RING

Words and Music by CLYDE OTIS
and VINCENT CORSO

273

YOU DECORATED MY LIFE

Words and Music by DEBBIE HUPP
and BOB MORRISON

YOU NEEDED ME

Words and Music by RANDY GOODRUM

279

YOU'RE MY EVERYTHING

Words and Music by J.M. de SCARANO,
N. SKORSKY and L. GOMEZ

YOUR SONG

that I put down in words. How won-der-ful life is while you're in the world.

7.8. I hope you don't mind, I hope you don't mind that I put down in words, How won-der-ful life is while you're in the world.

you're in the world.

Piano/Vocal MIXED FOLIOS
Presenting the best variety of piano/vocal folios. Music includes guitar chord frames.

E BEST BIG BAND SONGS EVER 00359129
of the greatest big band songs ever, including: Ballin' The Jack • Basin Street Blues
oogie Woogie Bugle Boy • The Continental • Don't Get Around Much Anymore • In
e Mood • Opus One • Satin Doll • Sentimental Journey • String Of Pearls • and more.

ST BROADWAY SONGS EVER 00309155
er 70 tunes featuring: All The Things You Are • Bewitched • Don't Cry For Me Ar-
tina • I Could Have Danced All Night • If Ever I Would Leave You • Memory • Ol' Man
er • You'll Never Walk Alone • and many more.

E BEST COUNTRY SONGS EVER 00359498
all-time country hits including: Always On My Mind • Could I Have This Dance • God
ss The U.S.A. • Help Me Make It Through The Night • Islands In The Stream • and
ny more.

E BEST EASY LISTENING SONGS EVER 00359193
er 100 beautiful songs including: Around The World • Candle On The Water • Day
Day • A Foggy Day • I'll Never Smile Again • Just In Time • Manhattan • Strangers
he Night • and many more.

E BEST SONGS EVER 00359224
all-time hits including: Climb Ev'ry Mountain • Edelweiss • Feelings • Here's That
ny Day • I Left My Heart In San Francisco • Love Is Blue • People • Stardust • Sunrise,
set • Woman In Love • many more.

E BEST STANDARDS EVER Volume 1 00359231
Volume 2 00359232
wo volume collection of 140 vintage and contemporary standards including: All
Things You Are • Endless Love • The Hawaiian Wedding Song • I Left My Heart
an Francisco • Misty • My Way • Old Cape Cod • People • Wish You Were Here • Yes-
day's Songs • and many more.

ST CONTEMPORARY SONGS — 50 Top Hits 00359190
me of the best, most recent hits, featuring: Any Day Now • Deja Vu • Endless Love
ashdance . . . What A Feeling • I.O.U. • Islands In The Stream • September Morn
hrough The Years • You Needed Me • and many more.

ST KNOWN LATIN SONGS 00359194
abulous selection of over 50 favorite Latin songs including: Blame It On The Bossa
va • A Day In The Life Of A Fool • The Girl From Ipanema • Poinciana • Quando,
ando, Quando • Spanish Eyes • Watch What Happens • Yellow Days • and many
re!

OADWAY DELUXE 00309245
6 Smash Broadway songs including: Cabaret • Edelweiss • I Could Have Danced All
ht • Memory • Send In The Clowns • Seventy Six Trombones • Sunrise, Sunset •
To Remember • What Kind Of Fool Am I? • A Wonderful Guy • and many, many
re.

NTEMPORARY HIT DUETS 00359501
hit duets from today's biggest pop stars includes Don't Go Breaking My Heart •
dless Love • Ebony And Ivory • Say, Say, Say • You Don't Bring Me Flowers • and
re.

NTEMPORARY LOVE SONGS 00359496
ollection of today's best love songs including Endless Love • September Morn •
elings • Through The Years • and more.

's GOLD UPDATE 00359740
er 70 Hits from the 80's including: All Through The Night • Endless Love • Every
eath You Take • Fortress Around Your Heart • Memory • Miami Vice • One Night In
ngkok • Sentimental Street • What's Love Got To Do With It • Total Eclipse Of The
art • and more!

LDEN ENCYCLOPEDIA OF FOLK MUSIC 00359905
iant collection of more than 180 classic folk songs including songs of true love, un-
uited and false love, spirituals, songs of the west, jolly reunions, international
gs and singing the blues.

ANDMA MOSES SONGBOOK 00359938
eautiful collection of over 80 traditional and folk songs highlighted by the fascinat-
paintings of Grandma Moses. Features: America The Beautiful • The Glow Worm
oneysuckle Rose • I'll Be Home On Christmas Day • Look To The Rainbow • Sudden-
here's A Valley • Sunrise, Sunset • Try To Remember • and many, many more!

#1 SONGS FROM THE 70's & 80's 00310665
60 of the top songs from the Billboard Hot 100 charts of the 70's and 80's, featuring: Every Breath You Take • How Deep Is Your Love • Joy To The World • Laughter
In The Rain • Love Will Keep Us Together • Love's Theme • Maneater • Maniac • Morn-
ing Train • Stayin' Alive • and more.

150 OF THE MOST BEAUTIFUL SONGS EVER
Perfect Bound - 00360735   Plastic Comb Bound - 00360734
Bali Ha'i • Bewitched • Could I Have This Dance • I Remember It Well • I'll Be Seeing
You • If I Ruled The World • Love Is Blue • Memory • Songbird • When I Need You • and
more.

70 CONTEMPORARY HITS 00361056
A super collection of 70 hits featuring: Every Breath You Take • Time After Time •
Memory • Wake Me Up Before You Go-Go • Endless Love • Islands In The Stream •
Through The Years • Valotte • and many more.

60 CONTEMPORARY HITS 00361078
Featuring: September Morn • Somewhere Out There • Song Sung Blue • These
Dreams • Time After Time • What's Love Got To Do With It • You Are My Lady • and
many more!

SONGS OF THE 1920's 00361122
Ain't Misbehavin' • April Showers • Baby Face • California Here I Come • Five Foot
Two, Eyes Of Blue • I Can't Give You Anything But Love • and more

SONGS OF THE 1930's 00361123
All Of Me • The Continental • I Can't Get Started • I'm Getting Sentimental Over You
• In The Mood • The Lady Is A Tramp • Love Letters In The Sand • and more.

SONGS OF THE 1940's 00361124
Come Rain Or Come Shine • God Bless The Child • How High The Moon • The Last Time
I Saw Paris • Moonlight In Vermont • A String Of pearls • Swinging On A Star • Tuxedo
Junction • You'll Never Walk Alone • and more.

SONGS OF THE 1950's 00361125
Blue Suede Shoes • Blue Velvet • Here's That Rainy Day • Love Me Tender • Misty •
Rock Around The Clock • Satin Doll • Tammy • Three Coins In The Fountain • and
more.

SONGS OF THE 1960's 00361126
By The Time I Get To Phoenix • California Dreamin' • Can't Help Falling In Love •
Downtown • Happy Together • I Want To Hold Your hand • Love Is Blue • More •
Strangers In The Night • and more.

23 AWARD WINNING POP HITS 00361385
23 of the best including Don't Cry Out Loud • Flashdance . . . What A Feeling • Memory • You Needed Me • and more.

24 AWARD WINNING POP HITS 00361384
Featuring: Copacabana • Fire And Rain • Holding Back The Years • Longer • Michelle
• Piano Man • Sara • Stand By Me • Somewhere Out There • We Built This City • With
Or Without You • and more.

YOUNG AT HEART SONGBOOK 00361820
101 light hearted, fun loving favorites: Alley Cat • Bandstand Boogie • Bye Bye Blues
• Five Foot Two, Eyes Of Blue • I Could Have Danced All Night • Let Me Entertain You
• The Sound Of Music • Tiny Bubbles • True Love • Young At Heart • and more.

PIANO ALPHABETICAL SONGFINDER 72000004
Complete listing of the thousands of songs included in the Easy Piano and Piano/
Vocal/Guitar books. Song titles are cross-referenced to the books in which they can
be found. Available free of charge from your local music store. Or, write to:
HAL LEONARD PUBLISHING CORP.
P.O. Box 13819, Milwaukee, WI 53213

For more information, see your local music dealer, or write to:
HAL LEONARD PUBLISHING CORPORATION
P.O. Box 13819 • Milwaukee, WI 53213

1-88

THE ULTIMATE SERIES

This comprehensive series features jumbo collections of piano/vocal arrangements with guitar chords. Each volume features an outstanding selection of your favorite songs. Collect them all for the ultimate music library!

Treasury Of Standards Volume 1

A must-have collection of 100 of the greatest standards of all-time from A-I featuring: All The Things You Are • Bewitched • Bluesette • Don't Cry For Me Argentina • A Fine Romance • From This Moment On • Gonna Build A Mountain • Heartlight • I Can't Get Started • and more!

00361431 . . . . $17.95

Treasury Of Standards Volume 2

Volume 2 in a collection of 100 favorite standards from I-O featuring: I'll Never Smile Again • If I Loved You • It's Not Unusual • Just A Gigolo • The Last Time I Saw Paris • Look For The Silver Lining • Make Believe • Misty • One Note Samba • Our Day Will Come • and more!

00361433 . . . . $17.95

Treasury Of Standards Volume 3

The last in a 3-volume set, features 100 best-loved standards from P-Z including: People • Satin Doll • Smoke Gets In Your Eyes • Strangers In The Night • Sunrise, Sunset • That's All • Watch What Happens • Who Can I Turn To • You Don't Bring Me Flowers.

00361435 . . . . $17.95

All-Time Hits – 100 Favorite Standards

A super song selection, including: After You've Gone • Bugle Call Rag • The Christmas Song (Chestnuts Roasting On An Open Fire) • Drifting And Dreaming • Easy Street • Flamingo • Hello, Dolly! • If He Walked Into My Life • Ivory Tower • The Man That Got Away • Moonlight Bay • Notre Dame Victory March • Sentimental Journey • Sioux City Sue • Tenderly • Unchained Melody • We Need A Little Christmas • What I Did For Love • You Call Everybody Darling • more.

00361424 . . . . $17.95

Broadway Gold

100 show tunes from a wide variety of Broadway's biggest hits: Bess, You Is My Woman • Happy Talk • I Love Paris • The Lady Is A Tramp • Let Me Entertain You • Memory • My Funny Valentine • Oklahoma • The Rain In Spain • Some Enchanted Evening • When I Fall In Love • It Only Takes A Moment • Mame • Seventy-Six Trombones • Summer Nights • Till There Was You • Tomorrow • What I Did For Love • Silk Stockings • many more.

00361396 . . . . $17.95

Broadway Platinum

A collection of 100 popular Broadway show tunes, featuring the hits: As Long As He Needs Me • Bali Ha'i • Beauty And The Beast • Camelot • Consider Yourself • Everything's Coming Up Roses • Getting To Know You • Gigi • Do You Hear The People Sing • Hello, Young Lovers • I'll Be Seeing You • If Ever I Would Leave You • My Favorite Things • On A Clear Day • People • September Song • She Loves Me • Sun And Moon • Try To Remember • Younger Than Springtime • Who Can I Turn To • many more.

00311496 . . . . $19.95

Christmas

100 of the best-loved traditional and contemporary songs of the season, including: Away In A Manger • The First Noel • Hark! The Herald Angels Sing • The Holly And The Ivy • I Heard The Bells On Christmas Day • Jingle Bells • Joy To The World • Let It Snow! Let It Snow! Let It Snow! • Mary's Little Boy Child • My Favorite Things • Nuttin' For Christmas • O Holy Night • Rudolph, The Red-Nosed Reindeer • Silent Night • Sleigh Ride • Still, Still, Still • Toyland • We Three Kings Of Orient Are • We Wish You A Merry Christmas • and more.

00361399 . . . . $17.95

Contemporary – 60 Solid Gold Hits

60 contemporary smash hits, including: Candle In The Wind • Don't Know Much • Don't Worry, Be Happy • Faith • I Write The Songs • I'll Be Loving You (Forever) • Islands In The Stream • Kokomo • Lost In Your Eyes • Memory • Sailing • Somewhere Out There • We Didn't Start The Fire • With Or Without You • You Needed Me • much more!

00490289 . . . . $17.95

Country

Over 90 of your favorite country hits in one collection! Features: Achy Breaky Heart • Act Naturally • Always On My Mind • American Made • Boot Scootin' Boogie • Brand New Man • Crazy • Down At The Twist And Shout • Folsom Prison Blues • Hey, Good Lookin' • Lucille • Neon Moon • Southern Nights • Where've You Been • and more.

00310036 . . . . $19.95

Gospel

100 of the most inspirational gospel songs ever compiled, featuring: Because He Lives • Climb Ev'ry Mountain • Daddy Sang Bass • El Shaddai • He • He Touched Me • His Eye Is On The Sparrow • How Great Thou Art • I Never Shall Forget The Day • I Saw The Light • I Would Crawl All The Way To The River • Just A Closer Walk With Thee • Just Any Day Now • Kum Ba Yah • Lead Me, Guide Me • Peace In The Valley • Rock Of Ages • Sincerely Yours • The Sun's Coming Up • Take My Hand, Precious Lord • What A Beautiful Day • Wings Of A Dove • more.

00241009 . . . . $17.95

Rock 'N' Roll

100 of the biggest rock 'n' roll hits from 1954-1965: All Shook Up • At The Hop • Blue Suede Shoes • Bye Bye, Love • Chantilly Lace • Diana • Hello, Mary Lou (Goodbye Heart) • I Want To Hold Your Hand • It's My Party • Lollipop • Peggy Sue • Put Your Head On My Shoulder • Save The Last Dance For Me • Sixteen Candles • Surfin' U.S.A. • That'll Be The Day • True Love Ways • Wake Up, Little Susie • What's Your Name? • more.

00361411 . . . . $17.95

Singalong!

100 of the best-loved popular songs ever: Ain't Misbehavin' • All Of Me • Beer Barrel Polka • California, Here I Come • The Candy Man • Crying In The Chapel • Edelweiss • Feelings • Five Foot Two, Eyes Of Blue • For Me And My Gal • Goodnight Irene • I Left My Heart In San Francisco • Indiana • It's A Small World • It's Hard To Be Humble • Mickey Mouse March • Que Sera, Sera • This Land Is Your Land • Too Fat Polka • When Irish Eyes Are Smiling • and more.

00361418 . . . . $17.95

Jazz Standards

100 great jazz selections, featuring: Ain't Misbehavin' • All Of Me • Bernie's Tune • Early Autumn • A Foggy Day • From This Moment On • Here's That Rainy Day • I've Got You Under My Skin • Manhattan • Meditation • Moonlight In Vermont • My Funny Valentine • Route 66 • A Taste Of Honey • There's A Small Hotel • What A Difference A Day Made • You'd Be So Nice To Come Home To.

00361407 . . . . $17.95

Love And Wedding Songbook

90 songs of devotion including: The Anniversary Waltz • Canon In D • Endless Love • For All We Know • Forever And Ever, Amen • Just The Way You Are • Longer • The Lord's Prayer • Love Me Tender • One Hand, One Heart • Somewhere • Sunrise, Sunset • Through The Years • Trumpet Voluntary • and many, many more!

00361445 . . . . $17.95

Standards, Vol. 1 – 100 All-Time Favorites

Volume 1 of a 3-volume set includes classic favorite songs from A-I, featuring: Ain't Misbehavin' • Blueberry Hill • Careless • Climb Ev'ry Mountain • Edelweiss • A Foggy Day • Georgy Girl • Here's That Rainy Day • I Remember It Well • I'm Beginning To See The Light • many more.

00361421 . . . . $17.95

Standards, Vol. 2 – 100 All-Time Favorites

More favorite titles from I-S, including: The Lady Is A Tramp • Let Me Call You Sweetheart • Let's Get Away From It All • Lost In The Stars • Love Me Tender • Moonlight And Roses • My Favorite Things • My Heart Belongs To Me • Never On Sunday • Nice Work If You Can Get It • The Object Of My Affection • Opus One • Pennies From Heaven • more.

00361422 . . . . $17.95

Standards, Vol. 3 – 100 All-Time Favorites

The last of the three-volume set features favorite titles S-Y: September Song • Smile • Songbird • What Kind Of Fool Am I ? • The Sound Of Music • This Is All I Ask • A Walk In The Black Forest • more

00361423 . . . . $17.95

FOR MORE INFORMATION, SEE YOUR LOCAL MUSIC DEALER, OR WRITE TO:

HAL•LEONARD
CORPORATION

7777 W. BLUEMOUND RD. P.O. BOX 13819 MILWAUKEE, WI 53213

Prices, contents, and availability subject to change without notice. Availability and pricing may vary outside the U.S.A.

0495